The gendered organizational cu

Felicia Högberg

The gendered organizational culture in a Social Welfare Office

LAP LAMBERT Academic Publishing

Imprint
Any brand names and product names mentioned in this book are subject to trademark, brand or patent protection and are trademarks or registered trademarks of their respective holders. The use of brand names, product names, common names, trade names, product descriptions etc. even without a particular marking in this work is in no way to be construed to mean that such names may be regarded as unrestricted in respect of trademark and brand protection legislation and could thus be used by anyone.

Cover image: www.ingimage.com

Publisher:
LAP LAMBERT Academic Publishing
is a trademark of
International Book Market Service Ltd., member of OmniScriptum Publishing Group
17 Meldrum Street, Beau Bassin 71504, Mauritius

Printed at: see last page
ISBN: 978-613-9-45392-4

Managers' perspectives on the gendered organizational culture in a Social Welfare Office

Felicia Högberg

Supervisor: Ann Kroon

Examiner: Pia Tham

Abstract: The aim with this thesis was to explore how a group of managers in a social welfare office perceive the organizational culture when it comes to gender issues. The method used is semi-structured interviews with six managers in a social welfare office in Sweden. The main result of this study is that women and male managers, as two socially constructed groups, experience different realities in this gendered organizational culture. Reality is referred to the expectations, actions and consequences. These different realities were described as manifested in multiple ways. Firstly, the tendency that women and men, as two groups, engage to a different extent in feminine respective masculine behavior. Secondly, it is manifested in the mangers' perception that a lot of the equality work is something on the side and not really reflected upon in everyday social situations. Thirdly, women and male managers described different expectations, which will consequently shape the individual´s social role in the organizational culture.

Table of contents

Keywords: gender, management, organizational culture, structural perspective, the public-sector.

Author: Felicia Högberg, Gävle University. Email: hogberg.felicia@gmail.com

1. Introduction

In the Swedish society there is a strong desire for gender equality (Kullberg, 2013, p. 1493). This is portrayed in the Global Gender Gap Report (2013) which concluded that Sweden came in fourth place in the Global Gender Gap Index. Swedish legislation, requires employers to promote an equal gender distribution and assist employees in combining work, as written in The Discrimination Act[1] (SFS 2008:567). The Discrimination Act (SFS 2088:567) also states that different experiences, knowledge and values that women and men hold should be valued equally. As a professional social worker, one should advocate for gender equality as written by International Federation of Social Workers (IFSW, 2015). Another guiding document that a professional social worker should follow is the 3rd Millennium development goal which is to "Promote Gender Equality and Empower Women" (IFSW, 2015). The author's understanding is that social work is a profession dominated by women. Due to as stated by Statistics Sweden[2] (SCB) 2015, were the gender distribution among graduates with a Bachelor´s degree in social work in Sweden 2013-2014 was 13% men and 87 % women.

In general, the public sector is dominated by women and the private sector is dominated by men (Regnö, 2013, p. 13). This is referred to as the "horizontal division of labor" in terms of gender distribution. The labor market is also vertically divided, which is seen in the increase of men holding positions higher up in the organization hierarchy (*ibid*). The public sector, which is dominated by women, shows the same pattern as of the rest of the labor market which is that the number of men increase, holding higher positions higher up in the organization (Regnö, 2013, p. 15). With this stated women in the public sector, still occupy most of the management positions available in total (Regnö, 2013, p. 15 and p. 27). However, statistics from the sector levels only give a general picture and the gender distribution can

---

[1] Diskrimineringslagen
[2] Statistiska centralbyrån

greatly vary between different public institutions (Regnö, 2013, p. 27). In this study, research done from other Swedish institutions and other western countries are included. To connect this general research position, with the research question and aim, the researcher is conducting interviews in a Swedish social services.

1.1 Research aim

In the public sector the proportion of men increases and the proportion of women decreases in the senior management. The aim of this study is to explore how gender equality in a public institution is perceived from the perspective of managers themselves.

1.2 Research question

1. How do the managers describe different traits important for a manager to posses?

2. How do the managers describe gender work in their organization?

3. How do the managers perceive and describe expectations on female and male managers?

1.3 Historical background to present day research

Historical organizational research has not been connected to gender (Regnö, 2013, p. 16). Instead research has been done about male leaders and at the same time describing leadership as a gender-neutral concept. In Sweden in the end of the 1950s and the beginning of the 1960s women's working situation reached the research agenda. In this spirit, during 1970s and 1980s critics stated concerns about the lack of gender perspective within this research. During that time the research started to focus on female leaders. At the same time, most research about women in leading positions has been as numerical minorities in a male-dominated management context. Also the majority of research has been done within the private sector (*ibid*). As written by Regnö (2013, p. 17) there has been extensive research of the public sector however, not with the focus of leadership. This lack of leadership research was brought to light in middle of 1990s. A government funded investigation was initiated to map out and

4

analyze the distribution of economic power and economic resources among women and men in Sweden. In that research, initiative studies were directed towards female leaders within the public service and other women-dominated areas. Although, if one is to compare the gender theoretical research there exists in the context of male-dominated environments, the leadership research within women-dominated environment is still relatively unexplored and research in this area is needed (*ibid*).

As stated by Nobel and Pease (2011, p. 30) in the mid-1990s, men were encouraged to be an integrated part of the design, implementation, monitoring and evaluation of employment policies and organizational practices to enhance gender equality. In early 2000 the neo-liberal agenda made its way into many western countries labor laws (Noble & Pease, 2011, p. 31). This led to a move away from earlier decided agreements towards a more deregulated workforce. Nobel and Pease (2011, p. 31) describe this as a setback for women and the public sectors continue to be underrepresented by women in senior management. According to Kullberg (2013, p. 1496) this development pattern of NPM can be found in both Sweden and other countries. Berg, Barry and Chandler (2012, p. 211) writes that this macro-context is a major influence in shaping of the micro social relations, subjects positions, opportunities and constraints in organizations. An interesting notion is that NPM has led to a focus on individualism. This focus leads to more opportunities for some individuals, both women and men. As for example NPM has created individual winners, in social work women-managers have gained valuable experience to enhance their individual value in the labor market. Though, as some individuals, the winners, may benefit at the expense of others, the losers. This means that the neo-liberal agenda, enabled through NPM, focuses on individuals rather than collective groups. The individualistic neo-liberal focus silenced collective struggles such the struggle against gender inequality. Consequently this led to reproduction in hierarchies of inequality. This is the context managers need to operate in and clearly affects the managers´ ability to make changes in the organizational culture (*ibid*).

With this historical background many feminists, especially with a radical and structural perspective, have questioned the gender inequality in organizations (Nobel & Pease, 2011, p. 31). The feminists identify limitations in addressing gender inequality in organizations from both the individual focus (1970s) and from the policy and legislative approach (1980-90s). The feminists argue that old approaches do not question the masculinization of workplace

5

norms and the widespread acceptance of those norms that favor men. These norms leave the gender advantages of men in the workplace unaddressed and men "off the hook" for analyzing their own role in women's discrimination (Nobel & Pease, 2011, p. 31-32). A new focus has emerged where some researchers, with a structural perspective, focus on organizational knowledge that analyzes the consequences of stereotypical masculine and feminine behaviors. These behaviors are called *"doing gender"* and it is done by both women and men (*ibid*). Nobel and Pease (2011, p. 32) point out doing gender is not seen as a naive or innocent activity but rather a dynamic activity that strongly builds the gender order in the workplace. This is explained as women and men act using scripts that favor men's privileges and women's subordination. According to Noble and Pease (2011, p. 329) these results are still present day reality where men's interests dominate over women's, both subjectively and structurally. Doing masculinity is the present implicit norm that guides women and men's behavior, expectations and actions in the workplace. So the new focus of understanding gender in organizations is to study men and masculine assumptions and the way these are accepted by both women and men (*ibid*).

1.4 The public sector nowadays

During 1980s the economic resources of the public sector were significantly reduced (Regnö, 2013, p. 103). During the 1990s the public sector´s economic resource were further drastically reduced (Regnö, 2013, p. 193). During this time-period a market-economic perspective on leadership-models was introduced (*ibid*). Regnö (2013, p. 103) points out that this reorganization lead to flatter organizations with less administrative support systems. The reorganization also led to fewer numbers of managers and little money for manpower care (Regnö, 2013, p. 105). Furthermore Regnö (2013, p. 106) points out that the administrative support functions are often cut down since it may be difficult for the public to accept the reduction of staff that work directly with clients, to make room for administrative support.

In Kullberg's (2013, p. 1500) study male-managers expressed that being a manager involves a lot of overtime and poor working conditions. The positions of senior management in the social services are less attractive today than they used to be. According to Kullberg (2013, p. 1500) men give women access to male-dominated working areas only when a status reduction has taken place and the conditions in working environment have worsened. In the UK male

6

social workers did not want to enter a management career because it would prevent them from practicing social work (*ibid*). Kullberg (2013, p. 1500-1501) further points out that in the Swedish social services, managers claim that their main working tasks are of a financial nature, such as budgeting and control activities.. This may be another reason why male social workers do not want to advance to management positions as much as before (*ibid*).

Ely and Meyerson (2000, p. 125) define extra work as something one performs over and above one's formal work. Extra work leaves less time to do work that "counts" in the formal reward system. Examples of this work include recruiting, mentoring, committees, task forces and serving as role models for other staff (*ibid*).

1.5 Explanation of concepts

Human service organization is a generic term for organizations where professional social workers are likely to be employed.

Manager or *chefer* (managers) as stated by Regnö (2013, p. 18). Here a manager is a person with administrative management and political work within the public and private sector. This work includes making decisions, planning, directing and coordinating (*ibid*).

Professional social worker refers to a person who has least 3 to 5 years of university education with social work as their major. The Swedish term is *socionom*.

Social services as stated by Kullberg (2013, p. 1497) is the biggest working area for social workers in Sweden. Social services is refers to *Socialtjänsten* in Sweden and is located within the public sector *(ibid)*.

1.6 Why this should be a concern for social work

Male privilege is evident especially in women-dominated institutions such as human service organizations (Noble & Pease, 2011, p. 29). This due to the absence of women from senior management and policy making positions, even though women have a numerical majority (*ibid*). Kullberg (2013, p. 1492-1493) writes there exist many studies were researchers have

7

concluded that men in women-dominated professions become managers to an greater extent than women. Even though, right now there is a vital decrease of the proportion of men occurring in senior management in the social services (Kullberg, 2013, p. 1492). Kullberg (2013, 1498) points out in the Swedish public sector, women now dominate the positions at case-handling, first-line and middle-management levels. At the same time, men are still overrepresented in senior management levels in the municipal sector (*ibid*).

Regnö (2013, p. 14) discuss that both the horizontal and vertical division in the labor market has consequences for people's lives. Such as in the top of the organization hierarchs men, due to their privileges, access greater influence (*ibid*). In The Discrimination Act (SFS 2088:567) it is written that employers are prohibited from discriminating among employees on the grounds of their gender, gender identity, sexual orientation, ethnic membership, religion or belief, disability or age. As written by The Discrimination Act (SFS 2088:567) employers that do not actively work towards gender equality are committing an offence against the law. The general perception, as in line with the law, is that the men's dominance in leading positions are problematic and an equality problem (Regnö, 2013, p. 15).

Gender equality is not just an issue important in the eyes of Swedish law and international human rights declarations and conventions. International Federation of Social Workers (IFSW) has member organizations in Sweden where national codes of ethics were adopted (Akademiker förbunder SSR, 2006, p. 7). Here the essential basis of the social workers ethics is human worth and the attached principle of human dignity. Human dignity is the equal and high worth of all human beings. Human dignity is simply inherent and is not dependent on the existence of a person's status in society. Essentially the point is to show respect for every human being and to take responsibility for one's own and clients life. Each client is allowed equal care and influence and naturally any kind of discrimination is discouraged (*ibid*).

2. Previous research and analytical framework

The literature and the articles were collected from the university library in Gävle and from databases accessed through the University of Gävle library website, namely Discovery and SocIndex. The literature and the articles about the methodology were taken from international social work course literature and from the University of Gävle library. The statistics were obtained through email-conversations[3] with the Human Resource-manager from the social services under study and from the SCB[4]. To avoid duplication in research, the researcher searched and has not yet found this study done. Therefore the researcher argues that this study can contribute to the organizational research span. From the previous research the author found the majority of theories and concepts she will use in the analytical framework. For that reason, this section will start with the general previous research. After that the researcher will clarify which exact theories and concept she will use in her analytical framework. To make the text easy to read, the researcher divided the previous research under six headings. After that she will summarize, under an own heading, the analytical framework. Why the researcher chooses to have both previous research and the theoretical framework under the same headline is due the close connection between them.

2.1 Minority-majority position

Some researchers and theorist claim that men, in women-dominated areas, such as social work, have an advantage in the recruitment- and reward situations (Dahlkild-Öhman & Eriksson 2013, p. 93; Wahl, et al., 2011, p. 168). On the other hand, women in men dominated areas, are discriminated against in the same situations (*ibid*). In many cases the greater the dominance of women, is the more obvious preference for men exists in these organizations (Nobel & Pease, 2011, p. 26; Wahl, et al., 2011, p. 168;).

This phenomenon will then continue to assist male over-repressiveness in senior management positions (*ibid*). How these statements relate to the present study is that men are a numerical minority in the organization in total but at the same time men are the majority in the senior management (SCB, 2015). As further evaluated by Dahlkild-Öhman and Eriksson (2013, p. 93) a numerical minority usually has a disadvantageous position. Still, due others state may to the structural patterns of men´s dominance and women´s subordination in society in general, this leads to a very different meaning of being the only man among women or being the only

---

[3] Researcher interacted with the Human Resource-manager through mail, in order to protect the anonymity of the research participant the author do not provide an link to the exact email-conversation.
[4] See reference list for the exact link for the table.

woman among men (*ibid*). Simply put, as written by Regnö (2013, p. 112), men advance easier in women dominated organizations than women co-workers.

2.2 Gender and doing gender

Since the author has chosen social constructionism as her philosophy of science she found that the social process amongst humans is of interest when studying organizational culture. As stated by Alvession and Sköldberg (2009, p. 24) reality is seen as an "ongoing human product". To start, *Gender* is defined as a system of oppressive relations reproduced in and by social practices (Ely & Meyerson, 2000, p. 106). As written by Ely and Meyerson (2000, p. 113-114) gender consists of social relations where the categories women and men, feminine and masculine, acquire its meaning and shape experience. These categories are influenced by specific social, political, and historical conditions. These categories are also influenced by other social relations such as class, race, ethnicity, nationality, religion, age and sexual identity. Gender is not something static or universal but rather socially constructed. Furthermore, *doing gender* (or gendered social practices) is the social relations that constitute gender, which are manifested in social practices. These social practices may either preserve or challenge the men´s predominance and women´s subordination. One way to study gendered social practices is to study informal work practices, norms and patterns of work (*ibid*). These statements relate to the present study due to the fact these theories place the participant´s statements in a bigger structure, namely the gender structure. This is done in order to discuss the empirical data[5] to see if patterns of doing gender, and in that case how, are evident in the organizational culture.

According to several theorists, both women and men engage in gendered performance, namely doing gender and are creators of the upholding of men (Berg, Barry & Chandler 2012, p. 407; Dahlkild-Öhman & Eriksson, 2013, p. 97; Regnö, 2013, p. 233). These gendered performances are described as influenced by one's position within the organization, past experiences and present work situation (Dahlkid-Öhman & Eriksson, 2013, p. 86).

How this argument is connected to this study is that the researcher chooses to study both women and men. She argues that the organizational culture is a creation of both women and men. An example of doing gender can be found in a study by Wahl et al. (2011, p. 169) where

---

[5] Refers throughout the study to the researcher's own interviews

interviewed women (in women dominated professions) had a positive outlook on their male colleges but at the same time were a bit ambivalent. The interviewed women expressed ambivalence due to the easy way men had when advancing within the profession. However, this ambivalence did not create a negative working climate for men, which it had done for women in men-dominated professions (*ibid*). Dahlkild-Öhman & Eriksson (2013, p. 93) point out that subordinated women may use irony to make the dominate person's privilege of interpretation visible. Ely and Meyerson (2000, p. 127) mention that doing gender has different rewards and punishments for men and women when not behaving in a traditional masculine or feminine manner.

2.3 Civilized oppression, doing privilege and internalized male chauvinism

Nobel and Pease (2011, p. 32), discuss *"civilized oppression"* to show the process of how oppression is normalized into the everyday organizational culture. Civilized oppression is rooted in culture norms and bureaucratic institutions where many of these practices are accustomed and subconscious. Privilege here refers to conforming to the masculine norm, which is white, western men (*ibid*). Mullaly (2010, p. 25) states that people that are suffering from injustice are often due to ordinary people that do not understand themselves as having unearned privileges and oppressing others. To practically act upon privilege is referred to as *"doing privilege"*. Nobel and Pease (2011, p. 33) states men as a part of the privileged group can easily ignore or not see how others, especially women, are deprived of the same opportunities. Through this subconscious behavior, namely doing privilege that men engage in, leads to reproduction of patriarchal social processes and structures. By making men's privilege more visible, civilized oppression will also become visible (*ibid*). How this argument is connected to the present study is due to the researcher arguing that oppressive structures can be enacted in a subtle manner in the organizational culture. If the certain groups do not see themselves as suppressive (or even are consciously unaware) it may be difficult to argue for the existence of oppressive structures. However, by making these oppressive processes visible it is then possible to study and question these structures.

As written above, doing gender is enacted by both women and men. The author chose to bring up the concept of *internalized and absorbed male chauvinism* in order to point out that women are also responsible for constructing the gender order in the organizational culture

(Regnö, 2013, p. 77). Internalized and absorbed male chauvinism is defined as women in women-dominated groups who internalize negative perceptions of themselves. This means that social subordination can be expressed and recreated in groups of women through negative treatment and negative feelings among each other. The group occupying the dominate position create the dominant reality perception. The subordinate group then needs to internalize and assimilate to the dominant group's reality perception. This is because the subordinate group uses the dominant group's perception to reach well-being in the organization (*ibid*).

Lastly, as mentioned by Nobel and Pease (2011, p. 36) if men still benefit from their "knapsack of privilege", especially in traditionally women-dominated areas, men will continue to be over-represented in senior management. Nobel and Pease (2011, p. 34) states that the dominant view is that the conditions in the human services organizations are simply mirrors of the patriarchal structures in the wider society. This argument is central to the fact the author argues that society's different structures will be expressed in the organizational culture.

2.4 Colonization of the feminine

Wahl (2014, p. 134) discuss of when women occupy most management positions, the construction of gendered management changes. Gendered hierarchies can occur through a colonization of the feminine, as more feminine practices and values are brought into the masculine domain (Wahl, 2014, p. 135). When a trait that traditionally has been coded as gendered feminine becomes significant and high-status its meaning changes and the trait becomes coded as masculine (*ibid*). An example of ***colonization of the feminine*** is from Wahl and Linghag´s (2013, p. 140) study where the interviewees pointed out the importance of emotional and person-orientated in senior management. Traditionally, being emotional is considered feminine. The trait emotionality here becomes acknowledged as important and the trait then became male-gendered. Wahl and Linghag (2013, p. 140) interpret this as men having more allowances than women for being different in relation to the traditional prevailing masculine management ideal. This is due to the dominant position of men in the management structure (*ibid*). How this observation relates back to the present study is in terms of the understanding that traditional feminine and masculine notions change over time.

12

Why change occurs in the organizational culture is interesting to study. What are the power relations behind these changes?

2.5 The New Man

The New Man is a concept that emerged in the Swedish context in the late 1960s (Kullberg, 2013, p. 1494). This concept was introduced partly to strengthen professional working women and to strengthen men's responsibility for children and home (*ibid*). Dahlkild-Öhman and Eriksson (2013, p. 90) states that generally a new management style that conforms to the concept of *the New Man* is on rise in Sweden. The New Man may lead to a relative dominance of men and subordination of women in the modern Nordic countries. This is explained by Dahlkild-Öhman and Eriksson (2013, p. 91) as; "The New Man is thus constructed as less patriarchal, but still masculine man, displaying an acceptable degree of dominance." This argument is of interest in this study due to the fact that traditional, authoritarian dominance may not be accepted well within a Swedish public institution. Rather, domination that is expressed, in a subtle manner might be interested to study.

2.6 Glass ceiling versus glass escalator

Wahl et. al. (2011, p. 168) writes that a classic concept in organizational research is *glass ceiling*. Glass ceiling is a negative construction that excludes women in male-dominated professions from advancing to senior positions (*ibid*). In contrast, another known concept is the *glass escalator*, a positive construction, which means a glass escalator pushing men in women-dominated profession up in in their profession (Kullberg, 2013, p. 1493; Whal et al., 2011, p. 168). Wahl, et al. (2011, p. 168) gives an example of glass escalator is men who described they were pushed into special areas, namely areas of more prestige and better paid, which were seen as more suitable for men. In the case of social work, men were expected to work with administration and planning, namely management (*ibid*). However, as stated by Kullberg (2013, p. 1493) this pattern is now in a change process. This change process is shown by women in the UK who increasingly become managers in the social services (*ibid*). This argument is relevant to this study because these subtle social processes may influence how the managers act within the organizational culture. In this study the men that are mangers are actually in a minority position and therefore the researcher found these particular theories central.

Nevertheless, as argued by Wahl, et al., (2011, p. 169) not only glass ceilings can have negative consequences, so may the glass escalator for men. Wahl, et al. (2011, p. 170) gives the example of male social workers were seen as feminine and passive. These negative stereotypes contributed to men changing their behavior so as not to be accused of some kind of sexual assaults, especially when working with women and children. The men experienced these negative stereotypes as very uncomfortable, it undermined their self-esteem and at the same time they questioned their choice of profession (Regnö, 2013, p. 79; Wahl, et al., 2011, p. 170). The author finds this argument central because one can see that gender inequality, or more specifically gender expectations have negative consequences for both women and men. In this study, one male manager brought up his experience when working as a social worker with children (please see "results and analyzes").

2.7 Analytical framework

To start this section the author will first bring up the broader approach from which she chose to view the empirical data. *Structural approach* as discussed by Mullaly (2010, p. 24) has the perspective of social structures, present within organizations, as major sources of oppression. Due to the fact organizations were created and are primarily still dominated by one particular group; bourgeois, Christian, heterosexual men of European origin. Consequently the social structure reflects and reinforces the assumptions, views, needs, values, culture, and social position of this dominant group (*ibid*). Mullaly (2010, p. 25) writes that the dominant group access certain privileges at the expense of other groups in society; people of color, the working class, non-Christians, gays, lesbians and bisexual, and women, etc. The social structures are imbued with racism, sexism, patriarchy, and classism which lead to one dominant group occupying more political, social, and economic power over the subordinate group. For example, dominance of men over women or white people over persons of color. These social structures have become internalized into the structures of society and hence become natural and subconscious in the roles, rules, policies, and practices in the organization (*ibid*). Since this study is connected to gender the author has chosen to include the *gender perspective* in the structural approach. Ely and Meyerson (2000, p. 107) states that gender is a

14

system of oppressive relations, which are reproduced in and by social practices. The practical actions, thoughts and social processes of gender in this research is referred to as *doing gender*. Doing gender are the social processes of the gender relations practiced by both women and men. Social practices are constructed by and for white, heterosexual, class privileged men. This practices appear as gender neural but is rather fixed and ranked oppositions (*ibid*). These points are central because this is the focus on the study. In order to studying the managers experience of gender equality within the organizational culture.

Secondly, the researcher understands that there are many definitions of organizational culture. Consequently one needs to chose one of these definitions, which can be viewed as an operational definition, in order to create focus in study and measurement. It is important for operational definitions to be clear if associations are claimed to exist of any phenomena (Payne & Payne, 2004, p. 234). The *organizational culture* defined by Edgar H. Schein (1992, p. 9) as; "a pattern of shared basic assumptions that the group learned as it solved its problems of external adaptation and internal integration, that has worked well enough to be considered valid and, accordingly, to be taught to new members as the correct way to perceive, think, and feel in relation to those problems."

Moreover, now the specific theories and concepts that are found in previous research, will be summarized in connection to this particular study. First, the theory of *man-glorification*, where it is possible for men in minority to have superior positions over women that are in the majority. Second, *civilized oppression* will also be used to understand subtle dominance within the organizational culture. Third, *doing privilege* will be looked upon in order to understand men´s privilege and how men are practicing these privileges. Fourth, *colonization of the feminine* will be included in the analytical framework due to the fact that it provides an explanation to why management styles changes. The author argues the importance of study and analyzing why change occurs in the organizational culture. Due to the fact if management styles change, will then the dominate power structures also change? Or is the change not really a change but just the dominate power structure with new packaging? Fifth, *the New Man* concept will be brought up due to the fact it can offer an explanation in how men can act within dominance without being perceived as dominate. The researcher argues that to act with traditional authoritarian dominance is not really successful in any social gathering in Sweden. Therefore, one needs instead to study the more subtle social processes of dominance that may occurring. Sixth, the concept of **glass ceiling** and **glass escalator** may be interesting to look at. In this study the researcher has focused on men, masculinity and masculine assumptions and therefore to analyze the social processes, riding a glass escalator, and how the patriarch structures are occurring. To conclude, the eight concepts or theories that have been used are generally because they offer explanations to the present gendered order in the organizational culture connected to the structural perspective. The researcher argues that in order to properly analyze any social phenomena, one needs ask which of the structures are behind any given phenomena.

3. Methodology

The content of the methodology section is nine headings, first heading is the philosophy of science which is social constructivism. Since this study is about the organization and the organizational culture within it, the author will try, according with social constructivism, to understand what actually an organization is. The second heading is research design, here the method which is semi-structure are interviews introduced. Also under this heading a summary of the gender distribution in the social services will be brought up. The third heading is about how the selection of research participants was made. The next heading is about how the empirical data are transcribed and which style of transcription used. The fifth heading is about how the empirical data were analyzed, and which are the practical steps the researcher took. Next headings are essay credibility; validity and reliability, where the trustworthiness of the research are discussed from different angles. The last heading is ethical considerations where the researcher tries to summarize the most important ethical standpoints of this research.

To mention briefly, the researcher found investigating the **narratives** is a good way to study the organizational culture. As stated by Ely and Meyerson (2000, p. 117) narrative stories may take oppressive forms and support the dominant organizational culture. These narratives then remain unacknowledged and unquestioned. Narratives are not just stories but they are also social practices that are a part of the construction of the social reality (*ibid*).

3.1 Philosophy of Science: Social constructivism

The author finds social constructivism a suitable philosophy of science since the objective of the study is to get an understanding of the experienced organizational culture. As stated by Alvesson and Sköldberg (2009, p. 23) the organizational culture consists of multiple social processes and the sense humans make of these processes. In this study the interviewees are viewed as active participants in these social processes. As stated by Alvesson and Sköldberg (2009, p. 23) social constructionism are a very broad and multi-layered perspective. Reality is not seen as something naturally given, rather as socially constructed. The experiences of a human's *self* is developed through interaction with other humans. Reality is therefore an "ongoing human product" (Alvesson & Sköldberg, 2009, p. 24).

Alvesson and Sköldberg (2009, p. 26) states that an important term concerning institutions and organizational culture is *institutionalization*. Institutionalization is the process in which an institution develops and exists. The creation of institutions are a matter of forming habits and routines (*habitualization*) which happens constantly when humans are interacting. Within this process of habitualization certain humans are expected to carry out certain actions (*ibid*). These statements are of importance to the study because of the fact that the existence of organizations (and naturally the organizational culture within it) are creations of humans. Consequently humans themselves are the ones that are supposed to act, to challenge theirs and others roles, in order to question oppressive structures in it.

Alvesson and Sköldberg (2009, p. 26) writes that humans create, within their social relations, new habits and routines in their actions. As a result new habitualizations may occur. In contrast, after some time the institution, which was originally created by humans, begins to be perceived as something external and objective (*externalization* and *objectivation* occurs). Alvesson and Sköldberg (2009, p. 27) discuss *alienation* which is humans become falsely separated from their action. A person's action falsely comes to be understood as something external to themselves (*ibid*). The author´s interpretation of this is the organizational culture (institution) may be perceived by their members as something that just exists "out there" independent of their existence (alienation). Rather than seeing the organizational culture as something created and uphold through their own and other humans action.

A central aspect of the institution and the organizational culture is the need for coherence and unity within the institution (Alvesson & Sköldberg, 2009, p. 27). Coherency is needed because it creates meaningful mutuality in the social interactions between humans. Again this process is an inter-human creation. Mutuality is important due to the fact it gives the institution logic and this logic assists legitimizing the existence of the institution (*ibid*). These statements assist the author to understand that the organizational culture can only exist if its members allow it. There needs to be some sort of agreement (mutuality) between the members for the existence of a certain organizational culture in the institution.

As written by Alvesson and Sköldberg (2009, p. 27) institutions and the organizational culture are created by humans (through institutionalization). This process of institutionalization is enabled by humans creating social roles for themselves and others. Roles are important for a human's creation of *self* since, through internalization, it leads to development of the self, a subject. So by playing one's role, the human participates in the socially created world. If the human internalizes one´s roles, the social world becomes subjectively real for the human (Alvesson & Sköldberg, 2009, p. 28). The author finds this argument important because it discloses the interviewees as active participants in the creation of their (and others) social role within the organizational culture.

To summarize, humans create and sustain the institution and the organizational culture within it. This is possible through relationally social actions between humans enabled through the creation of social roles. Hence institutions and organizational culture are not something separate from humans actions. The researcher argues social constructivism is a suitable philosophy of science due to that the members of the organization are seen as active participants in the creation of the organizational culture. This perspective sees that it is up to the members of the organization to change their social surrounding, not some external force independent of human existence.

3.2 Research design

In this study semi-structured interviews are conducted. Payne and Payne (2004, p. 131) describes semi-structured interviews as interviews based on a small number of open-ended questions. The answers are actively and freely explored by the interviewer for elaboration. In semi-structured interviews, subtopics are often used to assist the interviewer to concentrate on central themes (*ibid*).

Kvale and Brinkmann (2009, p. 84) stress the importance of seeing the interview process as a craft were the personal skills of the interviewer are essential throughout. The author find some inspiration from Payne and Payne (2004, p. 130), such as the interviewer needs to be polite and positive in general but does not try to establish any social relation to the respondents. This because it is both time-consuming and a potential source of bias for the respondents answers. Instead the researcher should try to stay neutral and not be demanding (*ibid*). Since the author herself is Swedish she could recognize and understand the meaning of certain expressions and sayings which are an advantage.

To comprehend the management structures, the author interacted through email with the Human resource-manager (HR-manager) from this particular social services. Bellow is an approved summary that assisted the researcher to find a focus in the study. The summary assisted the researcher because it showed, as in line with the research aim, that men are in majority at the senior management level in this particular social services. And this is the context the researcher wanted to conduct her study in.

Distribution in terms of gender among employees, the 29th of February 2015, accessed from the HR-manager. In total all the employees in the social services are 80, 4 % women and 19, 6 % men (total number of 342). Total amount of managers in all levels in the social services is 68 % women and 32 % men (with a total number of 26). The number of 1st line operations[6] managers is 18, were 88, 3 % are women and 16,7 % men. The total amount of branch heads[7] are 2 persons, were one manager is a women and the other manger is a man. However, the

---

[6] Verksamhetschefer
[7] Enhetschefer

trend turns here were the executive director[8] (which is one person) is a man. In the administrative board were the total number of person is 8, 3 are women and 5 are men. In the top of the hierarchy, in the head of local government[9], one person is situated, this position is hold by an man.

This study is qualitative in nature and the method used is semi-structured interviews using an interview guide (please see appendix 1). The interviews were primarily centered on this interview guide. Hence the interview guide from the first interview differs slightly from the last interview. The first interview is perceived a bit like a practice interview. This because the author was new to the craft of interviewing, but also because it was a trial of the research questions. Regardless, the majority of original questions in the first interview guide were kept. All the interviews were conducted in Swedish due to the fact that this was the working language of the research subjects.

In order to make the interviewees feel comfortable the author let them decide the location of the interview. All the interviews took place at the office of a manager or at a meeting room in the social services. The interviews lasted around 40 minutes and were recorded using an mobile phone. The information the participants received was given both through email days before and by a written letter of intent (please see appendix 2) at the interview occasion. The purpose of the letter of intent was to be ethically sound in the sense that the research subjects have an idea what they signed up for. The guidelines used are as stated Kvale and Brinkmann (2009, p. 71) to provide information about a study. This involves not giving too much information but at the same time not leaving out aspects of the research design that may be of interest for the research subjects well-being (*ibid*). The interview guide is made in order to meet the aim and research questions of the study. This guide is divided into five topics, where the interviews were directed to mainly follow. The themes were: Gender equality, Distribution in terms of gender, The gender-culture (könskulturen), Selection process when recruiting new managers and lastly Project diversity (Projekt mångfald). When asking questions connected to these topics the researcher always tried to keep-in-mind what Kvale and Brinkmann (2009, p. 131) stated that one of the most important elements is not to treat ethics as an separate part but as a matter embedded in all stages of the research process.

---

[8] Förvaltningschef
[9] Kommundirektören

3.3 Sampling: Selecting participants

The interviews were held in a social welfare office in a mid-sized city in mid-Sweden. The author chose to do the interviews in the social services where it was likely that the social workers would be employed, both as a social worker and as a manager. Due to the fact that the author does not have the resources to travel to other cities, all the interviews are conducted in one social services. Consequently, this had the advantage where one could dive deeply into one institution's organizational culture. Then respondents' experiences were all within one institution. On the other hand, to do all interviews in one place could lead to certain disadvantages such as the likelihood to generalize that may be more difficult to argue for, still, not the aim of this study.

The author was interested in interviewing managers at the senior positions and the sample was limited to asking a total number of 11 managers. The author wanted an equal gender distribution. As a result, three interviews with female managers and three with male managers were conducted. The author did not consider including different categories such as age, ethnical background, sexuality, ability or social class. The focus is in terms of gender when choosing research subjects. This may be a weakness as stated by Ely and Meyerson (2000, p. 120) whose experience with a white women and women with ethnic majority is of great difference than from an minority woman. At the same time, referring back to the research question and consideration that this study was done with limited sample, the author still advocates that an adequate study was conducted.

3.4 Data transcription

All the interviews were transcribed by the author alone, first transcribing an interview and then going back over the same interview again some days later to listen to the recording and make corrections to the transcript.

To increase the reliability and validity of the transcripts, they were sent back to the interviewees to make sure what the author transcribed was an accurate reflection of what the

21

interviewee had stated. At that time the author considered that the interviewee felt that the transcript was accurate and representative. The author gave, as stated by Kvale and Brinkmann (2009, p. 183), the research participants a chance to comment and discuss misunderstandings. After feedback from the participants, the author made some changes in the transcripts correct spelling errors and certain names. As expressed by Kvale and Brinkmann (2009, p. 186) the participant might have experienced shock when reading their own interview transcript. This, to some extent, is expressed by one manager after reading the interview transcript. The author considered the manager's feelings and responded by explaining the method of transcription and confidentiality. Despite this single occurrence, no other major changes were made, and the author received validation from all the participants regarding their respective transcripts. The style of transcription was written in a fluent way as stated by Kvale and Brinkmann (2009, p. 186). This was because it was easier for the research subjects to read. Naturally, the interviews were conducted in Swedish and translated into English. The researcher is aware that nuances in the quotations may have been lost in the translation.

3.5 Data analyzes

Firstly, the author went back to the research question and grouped the all the answers into central topics, which increased to eleven. The author wrote down statements from all the managers under each respective topic. It was during this phase one could notice the common and dissimilar statements or opinions. The author also grouped statements that were commonly expressed but also statements that were dissimilar from the rest. The researcher also added subtopics under each of the central topics were she recorded her own thoughts during the whole process. The eleven topics were chosen due to their similarities to the organizational culture (the research question) and to the interview guide. Since the organizational culture includes many aspects, a narrowing focus is made based on the interviews. Notwithstanding, the author considered to what extent certain issues were expressed when grouping the interviews into the eleven topics. Granted certain issues were expressed many times and they were included into one of the eleven topics.

After this phase, the author started to analyze the text by looking closely at multiple theoretical and analytical frameworks. This helped the author to construct three themes out of the eleven central topics. The theoretical framework was chosen because they provided structural explanations to the experienced organizational culture. The researcher consolidated the eleven themes from the empirical data into three themes that are in line with the theoretical framework. She did this in order to show that the patterns in the empirical data can be found in both previous research and in theories. This was done in order to clarify that structural patterns of dominance exists, even through in the practice it might be difficult to detect.

3.6 Essay credibility

As stated by Payne and Payne (2009, p. 196 & p. 233) the main aim of research is to obtain trust in the results. Trust must be based on rationale arguing that the research is an accurate reflection of the nature of the phenomena studied (*ibid*). As written by Denzin and Lincoln (1998:414) in Payne and Payne (2009, p. 196 & p. 233); "It is by recourse to a set of rules concerning knowledge, its production, and representation that it is possible to assert that we were faithful to the context and the individuals it is supposed to represent". Validity and reliability can be used as tools to assist the researcher to accurately report the phenomena under study (Payne & Payne, 2009, p. 196).

3.7 Validity

Validity means whether or not the method chosen measured what was intended to be measured (Kvale & Brinkmann, 2009, p. 327; Payne & Payne, 2004, p. 233). Payne and Payne (2004, p. 233) stated that validity includes the capacity of the researcher to encapsulate the characteristics of the concept being studied. The researcher needs to constantly check the credibility, plausibility and trustworthiness of the results throughout the entire research project to increase the validity of the results (Kvale & Brinkmann, 2009, p. 250). This can be demonstrated by giving a transparent description of the whole research process and demonstrate from where conclusions were drawn (Kvale & Brinkmann, 2009, p. 253).

23

To explore the organizational culture, the author found the method of interviews was suitable. To explore the norms and attitudes which encompass the organizational culture, a good option was to listen to the participant' reflections. Since the focus in this study is to explore informal and personal experiences of the research participants lifeworld, (not formal policies or opinions).

When Payne and Payne (2004, p. 234) discuss validity they mention *internal validity*. Internal validity refers to the study's own logic: did it achieve what was intended? Here the operational definitions should be clear. If associations are to be made, they should not exist in any unstudied aspect of the phenomena (*ibid*). This was done in this study by choosing one definition for *organizational culture* and basing the interview guide on that definition. This was indeed important because there are several accepted definitions of organizational culture.

To increase validity, the interview guide was first practiced with a project manager at a company (not the social services). Certain questions were then modified to really access the rich description and most central aspects of the organizational culture in the project. Practicing the interview also reduced the stress of the author. The first real interview, at the social services, was a bit of practice interview. As stated above, the interview guide was slightly modified in terms of including and excluding certain questions to fully meet the objective of the study, within the given timeframe. To reduce misunderstanding and to increase validity, the author asked follow up questions to clarify implied statements or unfinished statements

3.8 Reliability

Reliability as defined by Kvale and Brinkmann (2009, p. 245) refers to the consistency and trustworthiness of the research findings. Strong reliability can be verified if the results are reproducible at other times and by other researchers (Kvale & Brinkmann, 2009, p. 245; Robson, 2007, p. 71). Nevertheless, as stated by Robson (2007, p. 71) it is nearly impossible to do an exact repetition of the measurement when research involves humans. It is likely that the research subject and/or the situation were different in some manner (*ibid*). This may especially apply to research projects that have a more flexible design and use a methods that produce qualitative data (Robson, 2007, p. 72) (which is the situation of this study). This can clearly leave the reader questioning the researcher´s results. To counter this, the author has, as stated by Robson (2007, p. 72), included "thick" descriptions, such as quotes and detailed information about the research process.

A qualitative researcher views social action, or social processes, as being very complex and situation specific (Payne & Payne, 2004, p. 198). Social life is not stable and therefore the research cannot be entirely consistent (*ibid*). Despite that, to enhance reliability one can aim for having rational grounds supporting the study in order to accurately reflect the nature of what has been studied (Payne & Payne, 2004, p. 196). With this background argument the author herself tried to provide a rich description, arguments and explanations throughout the study. The author also tried her best to, as stated by Payne and Payne (2004, p. 197), make sure that all the respondents understood the interview questions the same way, to enhance the reliability. This was done during each interview by recording what misunderstandings the interviewees had of the questions, and by critical reflection after each interview.

To enhance the reliability further, the author used different wordings of the same question and similar questions to see if that led to different or contradictory answers, as written by Kvale and Brinkmann (2009, p. 245). This assisted the author to more closely understand the respondent's genuine thoughts (*ibid*).

3.9 Ethical considerations

The general ethical aspects the author choose to bring up for further discussion are informed consent, confidentiality, to critical reflect the on consequences of the interview and macroethics.

In the study it is included an *informed consent* (please see appendix1 and 2) which in this case is a spoken agreement and a written letter of intent. The interviewees gave their voluntary consent to participate in the interview. The author have recorded, with respondents permission, the interview is voluntary and they have the right to terminate their participation

25

at any time. The author also records when the participants states their consent to participate in the interview. In the letter of intent the author states her role as a researcher, the overall plan of the study, the structure of the interview, their right to be anonymous, the option to send feedback and questions after the interview and lastly the author's contact information.

To ensure *confidentiality* of the interviewees, namely protecting their privacy, their personal information are kept secret and the author are the only one knowing their identity (Kvale & Brinkmann, 2009, p. 73). However, this point the author have some difficulties to maintain since the managers has between themselves talked and therefore some of them knows which others who got interviewed. Despite that, when writing the results of the interviews the author ensure their anonymity by referring them as one big group, not point out individual managers. This due to that it may be more difficult to identify managers between themselves and to the public.

By *critically reflecting the consequences of the interview* one will be aware of the risk of harm to the participants as suggested by Kvale and Brinkmann (2009, p. 73). The author have reflected on the consequences for, not only the individual, the larger group they represent (Kvale & Brinkmann, 2009, p. 73). When critically reflect on this particular point the author have reached the conclusion that not any major discomfort come to the group managers for participating in this study.

What the researcher have been discussing above is what Kvale & Brinkmann (2009, p. 312) refers to as *micro-ethics*. To increase ethical considerations the author will consider what is describes as *macro-ethics*. The studies scientific interest or purpose might be used for a different purpose than it was initially created for by certain interest group in society. To deal with this matter the author are open to public discussion and input to what should be considered as social consequences and the possible use of the knowledge produced. Also ethical discussion can be initiating concerning whether the outcomes has been beneficial and to whom (*ibid*).

3. Results and Analyzes

4.1 Summary

Firstly, this study is conducted in a mid-sized city in mid-Sweden. The researcher chose not to disclose the city to further protect the privacy of the participants. The research subjects are all managers in the social services. The educational background of the informants vary, some are professional social workers, one teacher, one of cultural studies, others has single courses in social work and lastly one in public economic. So, some of the managers are professional social workers but not all.

The result indicate that women and men possess different expectations, exercise different roles, face different attitudes and consequently behave differently, from each other as groups, in the organizational culture. Of course managers should behave different etc. Still, the results point towards that the different reality and behaviors of the participants are due to the fact that they belong to different socially constructed groups, which are "women" and "men". The researcher do not point out individual managers, but rather study the organizational culture from the perspective of social groups. However, traditional authoritarian manners, are not found in the empirical data. Rather tendencies of more subtle pressures, social processes and behaviors guide both women and men are recognized. With the help of this particular theoretical framework one can recognize, analyze and study these subtle processes. The result and analyzing section are divided into three headings. Each of heading discusses in different lights the different reality women and men face and experience within the present organizational culture.

An commonly expressed opinion of the interviewees are that structures still affect the present day organizational culture at the social services. These answers are in relation to different aspects of both gender equality and the gender distribution in the organization. The structure has many dimensions, but the author discuss three themes, where the structure is manifested in different lights. The three themes are chosen due to the fact that they, as in line with present organizational research, focus on studying the dominating group, namely men and the masculine assumptions. Within each theme there are connected theories that aim to understand how these masculinist assumptions are experienced in the organizational culture.

The themes consist of the empirical data connected to previous research and the theoretical framework. To clarify the structural dimensions of the empirical data, the researcher brings up a statement of one participant; "I think that there exist structures the entire way, from which recruiting that takes place to what academic education people have". As a another manager express; "I think that inequality is a structural problem". With this two quotes the researcher want to clarify that the managers do have a structural awareness of gender. This structural awareness can be expressed in different customs such in the first quote discuss the general structures of society, are present in different areas, such as in the educational life. The second quote simply states that gender inequality is a structural problem. Why the researcher chooses to bring up these particular quotes is due to the fact that the structural dimension is expressed in some way by all of the managers.

To conclude one may refer back to, Nobel and Pease (2011, p. 34) which states, the situation in the human services organizations are mirrors of the patriarchal structures in the society. This argumentation is further discussed by Ely and Meyerson (2000, p. 115) which states that a particular masculinity is seen as the "natural" regime. This unquestioned regime is supported by deep-rooted structures and inequalities between women and men. These structures are often expressed in a subtle and indirect manner (*ibid*).

4.2 Theme 1: Femininity versus masculinity

How do the managers describe different traits important for a manager to posses (the first research question) is further being discussed here. One topic that emerged from the interviews is the notion about traditional feminine and masculine traits. The researcher asked questions about which traits are important for a manager to possess and summarized the answers in two tables. The author herself did the summery and categorization of the empirical data. She also named the traits feminine and masculine. To put it into words, women managers described, to a much greater extent than male managers, traditional masculine traits as important qualities for a manager. Male managers answered, to a greater extent than women managers, traditional feminine traits as important. Since the author wants to be transparent throughout the research, she has used the expressions of each individual manager in the summarized table below (translated from Swedish). This in order for the readers themselves to evaluate the answer in relation to the author's categorization. How the researcher categorized the empirical data is

28

strengthen with previous research, that discusses what actually traditional feminine and masculine qualities are. As written by Ely and Meyerson (2000, p. 124) traditional masculine traits are for example strong, assertive, independent, self-sufficient and risk-taking. Traditional feminine traits are for example collaborative, consultative, inclusive, non-hierarchical, supportive and concerned with relationships (*ibid*).

With this background the author want to show that, through categorization of the empirical data, that women and men, as social groups, tend to have different perception of a good manager. Naturally different perception of a good manager leads the two groups to adapt to a certain management style, in accordance with these perceptions. As written by Wahl (2014, p. 133) the constructions of masculinity change over time. At the same time the male norm in management, as ideology that service to justify men's domination over women, often remains intact (*ibid*). As expressed by on manager with a long career in the social services, in this study, discuss that the management style in the public sector have changed. Referring back to the table 1 and table 2, shows that management styles and the perception of important qualities for a manager changes. With this stated the researcher finds it of interest to study how subtle expressions of dominance are expressed and experienced. What are the reasons behind this pattern in table 1 and table 2? Before the evaluating on this point, the researcher wants to show the reader her categorization of the literal expression of the managers. So, is presented with the literal expressions of the managers, categorized by the researcher.

Table 1: Female managers' opinion what are the most important qualities for a manager

Tradition al femininity traits	Traditional masculinity traits
	Will to develop, not be afraid to say what you think, deal with setbacks, it is lonely, not to compromise too much, stand up for decisions and make well founded decisions
	Will to constantly improve, not be satisfied, to stand up for yourself, take fast decisions, have the attitude of "kamikaze pilot", dare,

	courage
Empathy, wanting to help people	Have a drive, wanting to have power, have the ability to influence, will to influence, curious, will to control, to have a control need, to be decisive, not to be too nice (traditional femininity trait) and not introvert (traditional women trait)

Table 2: Male managers' opinion what are the most important qualities for a manager

Traditional femininity traits	Traditional masculinity traits
Dialog-directed, not be too decisive (traditional masculine trait) and not have an attitude of I know best (traditional masculinity trait)	Process-directed, be clear and stand up in front of people
Create a good working environment, the staff should feel they have an influence and cooperation	Focus on the task
Good listener, prestigeless, don't have the attitude of you yourself always knows best (traditional masculine trait), flexible and reflect a lot	Take and stand for decisions and clear communication

To referring back to why this pattern in table 1 and 2 is occurring one interesting aspect is, there is an increasing recognition of building activities in organizations (Ely & Meyerson, 2000, p. 124). Traditionally building activities are seen as a feminine trait (*ibid*). Furthermore, due to the downsize in the Swedish public sector traditional masculine leadership capabilities are not seen as important as before (Kullberg, 2013, p. 1496). However, when these building activities are preformed by women they are ignored or sometimes discouraged. This is due to the fact that building activities are considered "natural" behaviors of women and are accordingly not considered to be a developed competency (*ibid*). Women that aim for advancement in organizations do so by assimilating to the primarily traditional masculine

30

organizational culture (Ely & Meyerson, 2000, p. 104; Wahl, 2014, p. 134). Referring back to the empirical data the researcher's interpretation is that women mangers may not engage, as to the same extent as their male co-worker, in traditional feminine practices due to the fact that then they do not get as much recognition as when they engage in traditional masculine manners. Simply due to advancement in to management, women may feel then need to exile from the majority of women and they do so by assimilating to traditional masculine qualities.

Then it makes sense for female managers to engage in traditional masculine manners, or? Actually, as written by Ely and Meyerson (2000, p. 127) women and men that do not conform to the traditional gender expectations are often treated differently. For example a task-oriented woman, a traditional masculine trait, are likely to be viewed negative. On the other hand relationship-oriented men, a traditional feminine trait, are not, but are rather celebrated. Further men that behave in masculine behavior is valued. So, women can be double-blindfolded when engaging in traditional feminine or masculine behavior. Blindfolded in the sense that engagement in traditional feminine manners they are unrecognized but engagement in traditional masculine behavior, they are regarded as inappropriate. Men on the other hand are viewed positively when engaging in either traditional masculine and feminine manners (*ibid*). The author's interpretation is that traditional feminine qualities are dominant in the organizational culture at the social services due to the clear numerical majority of women in the organization in total. As a result it is advantageous to absorb traditional feminine traits, especially for men, in order to advance in the organization. On the other hand, women that aim for management might have to conform, to some extent, to the traditional masculine management style, in order to stand out from the majority of women. Nevertheless, when women confront to masculine management style it might be problematic due to the fact that women may experience being "double-blindfolded". On the other hand, when men engage in traditional feminine behavior they may be viewed extra positively, because it is not natural for men to engage in traditional feminine behavior. Or when male managers engage in masculine manners they are not seen negativity. Men's positive responses and women negative response may be due to, as stated above, women and men are perceived differently when not conforming to traditional gender expectations.

Another interesting aspect one male manager brought up, is as manager it may be beneficial to act with gender neutrality. As he stated; "As manager, when you are sitting in the board you actually have to be more gender neutral". The researcher finds this statement interesting and start to reflecting why it is like this. As argued by Dahlkild-Öhman and Eriksson (2013, p. 90) leadership styles in the public area are in a change process. Change processes were more traditional feminine-coded leadership styles are replacing the traditional hegemonic bureaucratic masculinity. This new leadership style is *coded as both feminine and masculine* (*ibid*). By referring back to the theoretical framework the researcher try to understand this statement in the light her empirical data. Were, as stated by Wahl (2014, p. 140), through *colonization of the feminine*, traditional feminine practices become included in the masculine sphere. An example of colonization of the feminine is the quality of emotional leadership, which is traditional feminine, has been more common among male than women managers (*ibid*). Wahl and Linghag (2013, p. 140) state that why men can differ from the traditional masculine management ideal is due to that men have more space than women from differ from this ideal. This is due to the dominant position of men in management (*ibid*). The researcher´s interpretation of the statement of her participant is that there might is occurring a trend of change in the construction of a qualified manager. A construction that is not traditional masculine, but rather in line with traditional feminine manners. However, through colonization of the feminine these qualities are not prevised as feminine but rather than as gender neutral. Men may be more ease to assimilate to this "gender neural" management style due to the fact they have more space to differ from traditional masculine management ideal than women.

With this stated above, the reader might wonder both how the pattern both in table 1, table 2 and the change process of "gender neutral" management style, among men, are possible. How is this pattern and changes practically possible? Well from the researcher´s empirical data she did not find any tendencies of traditional authoritarian masculine management styles among male managers. Both the women and men interviewees expressed that there does not exist any macho-culture among the managers. Rather all the interviewees expressed that the climate among women and men, in the social services, as very gender equal. This statements got the researcher to reflect, even if is not a traditional authoritarian masculine style present, are there other means dominance can be practiced? Therefore, the researcher chooses to go back to the theoretical framework and the *New Man* discourse. As stated by Dahlkild-Öhman and Eriksson (2013, p. 91) the New Man is still an masculine man, but he shows it through an acceptable degree of dominance. This then it leads to continuation of men´s dominance and women´s subordination. Men may, by combining dominance, control with responsibility and flexibility in order to practice an acceptable level of dominance. When men are acting in this manner, both women and men may not perceive men's actions as expressions of dominance and gender inequality (*ibid*). The author´s interpretation of her interviewees is that male managers, may behaving as a "new man" and might exercise dominance without being perceived as dominant. This can be done consciously, or subconsciously or in somewhere in between. The enablement of the New Man discourse among the male managers is possible due to that they absorb traditional feminine qualities and consequently perceived as "gender neutral". To clarify the term gender neural, the author does not believe in such concept. Rather, through colonization of the feminine, male managers have adopted a traditional feminine management style and relabeled it as gender neural.

To conclude, there is a trend indicating that it is occurring a change in the organizational culture concerning the construction of a good manager. Should one behave in line with traditional feminine or masculine qualities, or both, to be a good manager? Well the researcher's empirical data shows that the answer of this question is different for women and men, as social groups. Women may experience difficulty when engaging in either traditional feminine or masculine manners. The empirical data indicate that women may still feel more bound, than their male co-worker, to behave in line with traditional masculine management ideal. The male managers are on the other hand are perceived positively when engaging in both traditional feminine or masculine manners. The empirical data indicate that male manager have adopted a rather feminine management style in order to be perceived as a competent manager. However, this feminine management style, or qualities, are no longer perceived as feminine but rather as gender neutral. This process occurs through the colonialization of the feminine. As a result, it may be formidable to change the male norm in management whatever form it will take such as in the New Man.

4.3 Theme 2: Extra gender work

The next theme is connected to how the managers describe gender work in their organization (the second research question) and consequently affected the informal gender work in the organizational culture. A big topic that emerged from the researcher's empirical data is all the managers agreed that their workload have great influence on their gender equality work. The researcher's understanding is that gender equality work is both a formal (included in one's workload) but also informal workload (not belonging to one's formal workload). As stated by many of the interviewees, nowadays as manager, one usually has a very high workload. A result of this information, the researcher will discuss the process of extra work attached to equality work and its consequences.

The HR-manager explained that when she was designing the Gender Equality- and Equal treatment-plan[10], she needed representatives to sit in the working-group for development of this. At the same time she mentioned that it was an issue to find representatives due to the fact that sitting in this working-group is extra work. She discusses why there was not so many employees signing up to sit in the working-group; "I have full understanding of this, due to that it would been extra work to sit in this working-group and one has already a lot to do". To further investigate this statement one need to put it in a context. As stated by Regnö (2013, p. 112) due to the cutbacks, managers may experience limited possibilities to question the working conditions. This may leave the managers only able to adapt the given framework for both themselves and their staff (*ibid*).

Kullberg (2013, p. 1500) discuss that the position of senior managers in the social services is less attractive today than it used to be. This is partly due to the status reduction and to the worsening of working conditions that has been taking place in social work. In the Swedish social services managers claim that their main working tasks are in the financial nature, budgeting and control activities. This may be a reason why male social workers do not want to advance into management as much as before (Kullberg, 2013, p. 1500-1501). To referring back to the researcher's empirical data, this context may be an explanation to the tendency that why much gender equality may be seen as an extra work and difficult to enact upon. Due to if the context within present public services are economically constrained, consequently the managers may experiences small possibilities to question the working environment namely the gender culture.

The researcher's interpretation of the empirical data is there exist an tendency that many times gender equality is an informal workload. At the same time, some equality work is a formal working-task, but still majority of gender equality work becomes an informal workload. In the sense that the managers do have certain frameworks of equality work (formal workload) but it is up to each individual manager to practically implement these structurers

---

[10] Jämställdhets- och likabehandlingsplanen

(informal workload). To practically implement then, in a way becomes an informal workload. In brief, gender extra work or informal work often, in practice, becomes something that the managers do "above" their formal working-tasks. The next paragraph shows further how managers themselves view gender equality work. Managers in the sense that they are not HR-managers and therefore have less formal equality work than the HR-manager.

As an illustration of the tendency of the high workload, one manager expressed how gender equality work may be experienced by other employees; "I can imagine that one thinks this is something to be treated on the side. As something "oh this, too" but it is about implementing this as something natural". This statement can be interesting to see in the light of Ely and Meyerson (2000, p. 125) statement that extra work is something one performs above one's formal work. Extra work leaves less time to do work that "counts" in the formal reward system. For example, this work includes sitting in committees, task forces and serving as role models for other staff (*ibid*). The author´s interpretation of this tendency in the empirical data is that equality work may be seen as extra work and not rewarded to a greater extent within the organizational culture. Staff aspiring to become managers may view gender equality work as extra work and not work that "counts", when one aims to advance. Equality work that is not rewarded may then affect the informal organizational culture to not prioritize this kind of work.

Further, this process within the organizational culture can be seen as a form of "*civilized oppression*". Nobel and Pease (2011, p. 32) writes that civilized oppression is an invisible and sometimes unconscious force. Men are seen as having unconscious privilege and by making their privilege more visible, civilized oppression can also become visible (*ibid*). To enact upon privilege is referred to as "*doing privilege*", which defines men, as a privileged group who do not recognize that they posses privileges and oppress others (Mullaly, 2010, p. 25; Nobel & Pease, 2011, p. 32). The consequences, as stated by Nobel and Pease (2011, p. 33), of civilized oppression and doing privilege prevents women from making valid contributions to work, and of reaching senior management. To connect these theories with the researcher's empirical data, gender equality work is seen as "something extra" by most of the managers. Further this process might not be recognized, as it might be a part of the civilized oppression and doing privilege, and therefor gone unrecognized in the organizational culture.

However, one manager, as quoted above, is aware that most of these managers view equality work as described above. With this awareness the individual manager can choose to behave differently. Nevertheless, the researcher´s interpretation, as tendencies can be found in the empirical data, is that most managers do see equality work as something extra. Consequently when managers view equality work as something extra, they separate oneself from the social processes that make up for the gender order in the organizational culture. Both women and male managers are a part of this process. Women managers, on the other hand, may subconsciously support civilized oppression, of themselves as social groups. But both women and male managers do not always recognize men´s privilege within this particular organizational culture. Rather, equality work is seen as something more "top-down", where the direction and actions for equality should come from higher positions in the organization, as expressed by many of this studies' interviewees. Instead, the researcher argues that the gender order is practiced and sustained, through everyday social processes, between managers themselves.

To conclude, the author´s interpretation of the tendency in the managers description of gender work in their organization, is that informal organizational culture is greatly affected by the formal structures of gender equality work. Gender equality work is mainly enacted into the organization as "something extra". It is not seen as something that is reacted, recreated and sustained by the managers themselves in their everyday social interactions. This may be an subconscious process, enabled through "civilized oppression" and "doing privilege".

4.4 Theme 3: Different expectations on women and men- lead to contrasting implications

How do the managers perceive and describe expectations on female and male managers (research question three) will further brought up for discussion now. One common statement of the interviewees is that women and men have different expectations on them and therefore are treated, and act, differently. Two female and one male manager have personal experiences of this. The three other managers did not express that they had been experienced being treated differently. At the same time, when the interviewees discussed more general circumstances, they all stated that women and men are in fact treated differently, in the social services office being studied , in the general society, or both.

One manager explained that as a social worker working with children, "You sometimes are asked how you manage due to that you are a man. Having supportive conversations with children. I had the feeling that you sometimes get questioned due to the fact that you are a man". Wahl, et al. (2011, p. 169) discuss mens´ low employment rate in certain fields, such as social work, did not depend on negative treatment from women colleagues or managers. Rather the men experienced being treated negatively in contact with people outside the profession (Regnö, 2013, p. 79; Wahl, et al., 2011, p. 169). For example, male social workers have changed their behavior when working with women and children in order to not be accused of sexual assault. When men were exposed to negative stereotyping and treatment, they felt this was very uncomfortable and questioned their choice of profession (*ibid*).

The author´s interpretation of the tendencies in the empirical data is that negative stereotyping of men, as stated by the interviewee above, may lead men to feel uncomfortable. This uncomfortable experience may further lead men into more perceived "legitimate" areas, such as management. Done in order not having to confront these negative expectations. Women, on the other hand, may not experience this negative stereotyping and do not feel the need to work in management for that reason. In short, the negative stereotyping of male managers, in this study, may have influenced the choice of career path to pursue a vertical career into management.

So far it has been discussed the negative expectations of male managers lead them into management. In addition, next will follow a discussion that illustrates the structural forces behind why men may end up in management, to a greater extent than women. One female research participant stated; "If you think structurally, I'm convinced that I have been treated negatively due to that fact that you are a women". She continued to explain that men tend to favor other men and as a woman you have the; "Responsibility to lift up and acknowledge other women co-workers. This because men do that for each other all the time". This statement may be interesting to discuss using the *glass escalator theory*. A Glass escalator occurs when men are pushed upwards in the organization hierarchy (Kullberg, 2013, p. 1493; Wahl, et al., 2011,p. 168). In social work fields, men can feel pushed into management, even though, this position have not always been their initial goal (Kullberg, 2013, p. 1493). The researcher´s interpretation of this tendency in the empirical data is that it is possible of the existence of subtle expectations of men to advance in the organizational culture. This tendency may be because a combination of both the negative stereotyping when interacting with certain clients and the existence of subtle processes of men help other men. The researcher interprets this tendency that when a man applies for senior management position there are other men who assist him in reaching that position. As shown in the summary bellow, the top-positions where strategic decisions are made, are dominated by men. This argumentation was also expressed by some of the interviewees in this study.

A last illustration of the difference experience of women and men, are the different expectations which can be summarized by one of the female managers. The female manager discuss that, women have different expectations than men and express; "I feel that women have higher expectations on them, like you need to be a bit better, as a female manager. Or I can also say that a male manager gets away with things that a female manager would not. Thus you need to prove more, you need to be more proactive, more driven and more competent". Her last statement can be interesting to see in light of Thompson and Marley´s (1999, p. 25) study discussing the survival strategies of women in human service organizations. One of the interviewees stated that, in order to be taken seriously as a woman and a manager, one needs to work harder and be smarter than a male counterpart to be considered credible (*ibid*). As stated by Wahl (2014, p. 143) women tend to over-achieve to prove that they are as competent as their male counterparts. Regnö (2013, p. 105) further states that women are more inclined than men to face ill-health such as stress caused by high expectations and small mandate. Previous research confirms that the patterns, in this study, of high expectations which women experience can also be found in other contexts. The researcher finds this both worrying and important to study why this pattern exists. One may look for explanations behind this statement above (this papers´ empirical data) by referring back to the theory of *"man-glorification"*. Regnö (2013, p. 232) describes man-glorification when men experience a greater leniency than women. Women and men are valued differently when occupying a numerical minority position. One can not assume minority of men at an organization will lead to subordination. Rather mens' privilege position, even if only a minority, contributes to gets a greater margin of maneuvering than the majority (*ibid*). On the other hand, Wahl (2014, p. 143) writes that women many times overcompensate to prove that they are as competent as their male co-workers. The author´s interpretation, of the tendency in this research, is that the women research participants in this study may feel the need to work harder and perform better than their male co-workers, as expressed by one women manager. This may be due to the fact the women may feel the need to compensate for their subordinate position in the in the organizational culture, as this tendency can be found in the empirical data. Womens´ need to overcompensate and mens´ leniency may depend on expectations. Women are expected to perform more than men (and some women may do that). The men might not feel these high expectations, due to that they are already occupying a dominant position, and instead experience greater leniency. Therefore it might be so that the dominant and subordinate groups behave differently due to their expectations in the organizational culture.

To summarize, the tendencies in this study show that female and male research participants possess different expectations and consequently different experience. This has many reasons but discussed here is that men may be exposed to negative stereotyping and therefore find management a suitable option. Another reason may be that men are riding a glass escalator which carries them into management. Lastly, due to different expectations, women might feel the need to outperform their male colleagues. On the other hand men may instead feel greater margin of maneuvering. This is enabled through the process of "man-glorification". Even through men exist in numerical minority and women in majority, the men are still the dominant group. The researcher interprets that man-glorification and men´s dominant position, when existing in minority, as a sign of the patriarch structures of society present in this study´s organizational culture.

4.5 Summary of the empirical data and the researcher´s interpretation

The main result of this study is that these female and male managers, as two socially constructed groups, experience different realities within the gendered organizational culture. Reality here is referred to in terms of experience, expectations, actions and consequences. The authors' interpretation of the tendencies is that managers' realities in social services, are social processes created by both genders. The different realities can be manifested in multiple ways. In the following paragraphs the researcher will summarize all these manifestations under the three themes.

The first theme shows the tendency that women display more traditional masculine behaviors, and men display more traditional feminine behaviors. The researcher´s interpretation of this tendency in the empirical data together with previous research is that different consequences occur when women and men engage in traditional feminine, respective masculine, manners. Women do not behave in a traditional feminine manner because it is seen as a "natural", or normal, behavior and therefore, not often rewarded. Therefore, female research participants engaged to a greater extent in traditionally masculine behaviors. Due to the fact women suffered from a structural disadvantage and therefore the female managers did not feel as comfortable as men to deviate from the traditional masculine management norm. In addition, in order for women to be different from the majority of women, one might adopt more traditional masculine traits. Therefore, women engage in traditional masculine manners and management styles. In the predominately female field of social work, the researcher´s conclusion is that men have chosen to adopt more traditional feminine behaviors. In this light, male social workers are seen more positively because they adopt a "natural" behavior, which female social workers are expected to have. Natural in the sense they are expected from women but not expected from men and therefore seen as a developed competency of men. Furthermore, due to men´s dominant positions, they are more likely to depart from a traditional masculine management norm, which was dominant before. Instead of assimilate to building activates, traditional feminine, which are now seen as more important.

A tendency exist that "gender-neutral" management style is perceived as beneficial, especially for male managers. The researcher´s interpretation of the empirical data together with theory is that change occurs in management styles. However, change is not a move towards gender neutrality, but rather a pattern of *colonization of the feminine*. In the sense that when a traditional feminine trait becomes important, the content of it stays the same but instead it becomes perceived as a typical masculine trait. Or as in this case, not consider feminine but rather something that is taken for granted and as gender neutral. The tendencies in the empirical data does support this theory as no masculine behaviors, such as a traditional masculine authoritarian management styles, are present. The researcher's interpretation of the empirical data together with the theory is that the male managers may have adopted traditional feminine traits, relabel them as a gender neutral management style, and practice this style with an acceptable degree of dominance. In other words, the "gender neutral" management style goes hand in hand with the New Man behavior.

The second theme, from the manger's perception is that there exist tendencies that working towards gender equality is seen as extra work. The researcher's interpretation of this tendency in the empirical data together with the previous research is that although gender equality work is a formal, and expected, part of a managers' workload, it often becomes a part of the informal workload. Because managers have a high workload, gender equality work is not always prioritized. Implementation, and the development of, official structures to encourage gender equality is many times up to each individual manager themselves. The economically strained situation leads managers to adapt a given framework for, equality work without maybe question it.

This "something on the side" thinking affects gender equality work in an organizational culture. The researcher's interpretation of this tendency in the empirical data together with the previous research is that this manner of thinking is further enabled when the organizational culture might not reward equality work to the necessary extent. There exist tendencies in the empirical data which indicate that gender equality work is not considered work that "counts" and therefore, not rewarded to a great extent. To further understand why gender equality work may be treated as something on the side, the researcher used the theories of *civilized oppression* and *doing privilege*. Adopting the attitude that gender equality work is "something on the side", the managers in this study have distanced themselves from the social processes in the organization. By not acknowledging the participation in these social processes, the managers are actually contributing to the construction of the present gender order in the organizational culture. Simultaneously, because of worsening work conditions and budget cuts, a tendency is that male social workers are not presuming management careers to the same extent as before. As a result, women may then access management positions.

The third theme is about the perceived differences between male, and female social workers. Involves the tendencies of the empirical data which shows male social workers can feel uncomfortable in some areas of social work, such as when working with children. The researcher's interpretation of the empirical data together with previous research reveals that negative stereotyping of men working with children, can be found in this and other contexts. This negative stereotyping may play a role in a male social workers' decision to advance into management. Another reason that men might be a part of an organizational culture is that men tend to help other men. In this study there are found tendencies which are inline with the

41

theory of the *glass escalator*. The tendencies in the empirical data indicates that there are subtle pressures for men to advance in the organizational hierarchy and that the glass escalator is enabled partly when men help other men to advance. The empirical data, indicates that there are different expectations for male, and female, managers. Women may face higher expectations, within the organizational culture, and on the other hand, men may experience greater margins of maneuvering. This means that male managers can get away with behaviors that a women co-worker can not. The researcher´s interpretation of the empirical data together with previous research is that this pattern exists in other organizational contexts as well. Although there are fewer male managers in total, they can have a superior position over the majority of managers, namely over women. This interpretation is supported by the theory of *man-glorification*. Man-glorification theory states that men experience a greater margin of maneuvering than the majority, that is women.

4. Discussion

The main result of this study is that there exists tendencies that female and male managers in this study experience different realities within the gendered organizational culture. Reality here is referred to in terms of experience, expectations, actions and consequences. The construction and sustainability of the present reality is a process contributed to by both women and men. With this stated the researcher argues that she has answered the research questions. Due to the fact that the researcher have now gained an understanding of the managers' own experience of gender within the organizational culture. Since the research questions is an open-end question that can include many aspects, clearly it can be further studied and evaluated. In the empirical data, one can find a tendency, namely women and men as two groups' possess different experiences. The different experiences may depend on individual alterations which is caused by women and men belong to two different socially constructed groups.

The consequences of this research are hopefully two aspects. The first aspect of this research is that it focuses on the dominate group´s, namely men, role in the gender order. To clarify, the gender order is contributed to by both genders, but to focus on the dominate group has

42

advantages. Due to the fact it may lead focus away from individualism and singularity, instead, to critical reflection on the underlying structures and view plurality instead. Another consequence of this research is showing how gender inequality is experienced and formed in one organizational culture. As the empirical data shows, gender inequality is often subtle and unrecognized. Consequently, it may be difficult to actually identify it within the organizational culture.

To further discuss the tendencies in the results one may look at previous research and the theories applied. Tendencies in this study can also be found in previous research. This led the author to the understanding that the tendencies in this research can be viewed with a structural, rather than individual, focus. Therefore, the use of these specific theories, which have structural points of departure, was seen as suitable. Still, as stated by Ely and Meyerson (2000, p. 142) no single critic is likely to reveal all forms of inequality people may experience. Rather a different focus will lead to different viewpoints (*ibid*).

With this stated the main goal of this research is clearly to contribute to increased gender awareness and equality between the genders in management. The researcher´s interpretation is that there exist tendencies in the empirical data which indicate that gender equality work in the social services is both a time consuming and an economically expensive project. The author argues that if change is to be made to enhance human dignity and the worth of every human being, one should think in a more unconventional way. As stated by Ely and Meyerson (2000, p. 132) in order to reach gender equality one should break down traditional constructions of male, women, masculine and feminine. This in order to enable a more fluid concept of identity in the organizational culture (*ibid*). The researcher argues that allowing both women and men to truly access the whole spectrum of feminine and masculine attributes will lead to enhancing the managers capability and positive effect in the organizational culture. This may lead the research participants to not only to become more competent and productive managers but to reach human fulfillment and well-being. As further discussed by Ely and Meyerson (2000, p. 132), the same process that creates gender inequality is also the same process that undermines organizational effectiveness. This is due to the fact that the unequal gender practices are upheld by beliefs of simply "this is the way things are". Consequently, this attitude led the staff not to question inefficient organizational processes.

Hence proficient equality work can contribute to improving the organization's effectiveness (*ibid*).

The researcher argues that the view of working for gender equality, traced in the empirical data, as rather something extra, something on the side, something that takes resources and time is not a beneficial perspective. Rather, the managers can instead choose to view gender equality as an instrument to question old, inefficient and unequal structures. How this can be practically accomplished by the research participants, one can draw inspiration from Ely and Meyerson (2000, p. 133) statements on organizational change. They advocate that change is reached not through a wholesale revolution but rather through localized processes of incremental change. Gender equality is reached through a series of interventions, namely resistance to disrupt the traditional gendered social practices in everyday social interaction (Ely & Meyerson, 2000, p. 133). The researcher argues that this perspective has advantages to the specific organizational culture studied. Referring back to the tendencies in the empirical data, gender equality work seems rather like an abstract gigantic project that more than a few managers found difficult to implement. By viewing gender equality work as something on the side, it is often ignored in the everyday organizational culture. Thus, with this alternative perspective, gender equality work could then be a natural part of the organizational culture. So if the research participants view gender inequality as a product produced by one's action, they are more likely to take responsibility for their actions. Consequently, when one takes personal responsibility for enacting gender equality, constructive solutions will follow logically.

5.1 Limitations of the study

To start with, this study is conducted only in one group in the organization and all the interviews are done in one organization culture. This leads to that the results can not be generalized. Another limitation is the experience of the researcher should be mentioned since the author is just a beginner in the craft of interviewing. As stated by Kvale and Brinkmann (2009, p. 84) the competence, skills, sensitivity and knowledge of the researcher can affect the quality of knowledge produced. Another limitation of this study, is what Ely and Meyerson (2000, p. 130) discuss as different aspects of the researcher's identity, such as gender, race and class. These will affect the perception and analysis of the social practice, namely the

44

organizational culture. This may be seen if an all-white research team analyzes gender relations by focusing on managers who also are all white. Their analysis of the gender relations in that organization will likely take white, middle-or upper-class experience for granted (*ibid*). This indeed has some striking similarities with the author's background. To deal with this, the author tried to constantly be critical questioning, and reflect on her preconceptions. To show this critical self-awareness the researcher tried to provide a transparent description through the whole research process. Once again it would be useful to actually conduct this study with a different researcher who can question one's interpretations.

The focus of this study is gender from the experience of white women and white men. Accordingly, this study has clear limitations for including multiple levels of inequality. Due to as stated by Ely and Meyerson (2000, p. 142) it is important to view reality from different perspectives, as creating a more comprehensive structure to see the different regimes of inequality in organizations.

5.2 Suggestions for future research

The author hopes that this study can act both as an informative study but also as an inspiration for future research. Due to the fact that the study is conducted in only one organization, a suggestion is to do the study in another context. Another suggestion is to do the study with an intersectional perspective which may lead to a comprehensive analysis of oppression. Nevertheless, the author argues to, as was done in this research project and which is in line with the research span of organization research, focus on men, masculinity and the masculine assumptions played out in the organizational culture. As presented in the result section, both women and men play an active part in the creation of the organizational culture. Therefore it makes sense to analyze both of the actors, namely not just women as in earlier research. A final suggestion for future research would be to further evaluate on the neo-liberal influence.

6. Reference list

Alvesson, M. and Sköldberg, K., 2009. *Reflexive methodology: New vistas for qualitative research*. London: Sage Pub.

Akademiker förbundet SSR., 2006. *Ethics in Social Work: An ethical code for social work professionals*. [pdf] Akademiker förbundet SSR. Available at: <http://cdn.ifsw.org/assets/Socialt_arbete_etik_08_Engelsk_LR.pdf> [Accessed 14 October 2015].

Bekhouch, Y., Hausmann, R., Tyson, L. and Zahidi, S., 2013. *The global gender gap report 2013*. Geneva: World Economic Forum

Berg, E., Barry, J. and Chandler, J., 2012. Changing Leadership and Gender in Public Sector Organizations. *British Journal of Management*, [e-journal] 23(3), 402-414.

Dahlkild-Öhman, G. and Eriksson, M., 2013. Inequality Regimes and Men's Positions in Social Work. *Gender Work and Organization*, [e-journal] 20(1), 85-99.

Diskrimineringslagen (SFS 2088:567). Stockholm: Regeringskansliet / Lagrummet.

Ely, R.J. and Meyerson D.E., 2000. Theories of Gender in Organizations: A New Approach to Organizational Analysis and Change. *Research in Organizational Behavior*, [e-journal] 22(0), 103-151.

International Federation of Social Workers, 2015. *Statement of Ethical Principles*. [online] Available at: < http://ifsw.org/policies/statement-of-ethical-principles/> [Accessed 14 October 2015].

Kullberg, K., 2013. From Glass Escalator to Glass Travelator: On the Proportion of Men in Managerial Positions in Social Work in Sweden. *British Journal of Social Work*, [e-journal] 43(8), 1492-1509.

Kvale, S. and Brinkmann, S., 2009. *Interviews: Learning the craft of qualitative research interviewing*. Los Angeles: Sage Pub.

Mullaly, B., 2010. *Challenging oppression and confronting privilege*. Ontario: Oxford University Press.

Noble, C. and Pease, B., 2011. Interrogating Male Privilege in the Human Services and Social Work Education. *Women in Welfare Education*, [e-journal] 10, 29-38.

Payne, G. and Payne, J., 2004. *Key concepts in social research*. London: Sage Pub.

Regnö, K., 2013. Det osynliggjorda ledarskapet: Kvinnliga chefer i majoritet. *KTH Royal Institute of Technology*, [online].

Robson, C., 2007. *How to do a research project: A guide for undergraduate students*. Oxford: Blackwell Pub.

SCB (2014) Antal examina efter universitet/högskola, SUN-inriktning (1-siffernivå), SUN-inriktning (2-siffernivå), examen och kön, läsåren 1993/94–2013/14. 2015 (September, 2). [online] Available at: <http://www.scb.se/sv_/Hitta-statistik/Statistik-efter-amne/Utbildning-och-forskning/Hogskolevasende/Studenter-och-examinerade-i-hogskoleutbildning-pa-grundniva-och-avancerad-niva/#c_li_76738> [Accessed 14 October 2015].

Schein, E.H., 1992. *Organizational Culture and Leadership: A Dynamic View*. 2nd ed. San Francisco: Jossey-Bass Pub.

Thompson, J. and Marley, M., 1999. Women in Human Services Management: Continued Issues and Concerns. *Administration in Social Work*, [e-journal] 23(2), 17-31.

Wahl, A., Holgersson, C., Höök, P. and Linghag, S., 2011. *Det ordnar sig: Teorier om organisation och kön*. 2nd ed. Lund: Studentlitteratur AB.

Wahl, A. and Linghag, S., 2013. *Män har varit här längst: Jämställdhet och förnyelse i industriella organisationer*. Lund: Studentlitteratur AB.

Wahl, A., 2014. Male Managers Challenging and Reinforcing the Male Norm in Management. *NORA: Nordic Journal of Women's Studies*, [e-journal] 22(2), 131-146.

6.1 Appendix 1: Interview guide

Börja inspelningen:

Att delta i denna intervju är frivillig och du har rätt att när som helst avbryta din medverkan. Ger du ditt medgivande att delta i denna intervju? (muntligt medgivande). Kan du säga ditt namn, position, kort om din professionella bakgrund samt hur länge har du jobbat som chef här?

Jämställdhet:

- Hur skulle du definiera jämställdhet?

- Är det viktigt med ett jämställdhetsperspektiv? Varför eller varför inte?

- Chefer kan be sedda som goda kandidater för ökad jämställdehet. Känner du, som chef, att du har ett speciellt ansvar att motarbeta könsskillnader? Varför eller varför inte?

- Hur bedriver du, som chef, jämställdhetsarbete för din avdelning du ansvarar för?

- Har ni haft någon eller några som direkt eller indirekt motsatt sig jämställdhetsarbetet? *Om ja: följdfråga: Vad var det som den personen motsatte sig emot? Var det en man eller kvinna?*

- Är det inte viktigare att ha ett individuellt perspektiv istället för att ha ett jämställdhetsperspektiv? Vilket menas att man borde fokusera på individens egenskaper istället för deras kön?

Könsfördelning:

Visa dem statistiken

- Totalt 80 % av medarbetarna är kvinnor och 20 % är män på socialtjänsten i Gävle. Dock i förvaltningsledningen är det är 37 % kvinnor och 62 % män. Vad tycker du om denna situation?

- Hur upplever du att jobba i en kvinnodominerande organisations som denna?

Könskulturen (normer och värderingar):
- Kan du beskriv kort din arbetsplats ur ett jämställdhetsperspektiv? *Följdfråga: Kan du beskriva "hur saker och ting fungerar här"?*

- Vissa arbetsuppgifter passar bättre män respektive vissa arbetsuppgifter passar bättre kvinnor *(pga. av socialiseringen).* Kan du ge några exempel på arbetsuppgifter som är bättre lämpande män respektive vissa arbetsuppgifter som är bättre lämpade för kvinnor?

- Hur skulle du beskriva organisations-kulturen bland er chefer ur ett jämställdhetsperspektiv? Är könsfördelningen bland er chefer viktig? Varför eller varför inte? *Följdfråga: Känner du att du passar in bland andra kvinnliga respektive manliga chefer? På vilket sätt?*

- Det är ganska vanligt i organisationer att kvinnor och män har olika chefs positioner det finns tillexempel det är ofta fler kvinnliga chefer inom HR samt enhetchef medan män ofta dominerar ekonomi och förvaltningschef. Varför tror du att det är så?

- Varför tror det finns mer män än kvinnor i de högsta chefspositionerna?

- Hur upplever du de nuvarande chefstrukturerna? Är de bra som det är eller något som kan behövas ändras?

- Låt oss säga att en kvinnlig chefs kollega klagar på att jobbet som chef är stressigt, är det inte då hennes egna ansvar att förbättra hennes situation? Inte socialtjänstens "problem".

Till kvinna:

1. Anser du att kvinnliga chefer har ett speciellt ansvar att representera andra kvinnor? Varför eller varför inte?

2. Varför tror du att det **inte** finns fler kvinnor inom de höga chefs-positionerna?

3. Har du någon gång upplevt några hinder för att du är kvinna?

Till man:

1. Anser du som man att kvinnliga chefer har ett speciellt ansvar att representera andra kvinnor? Varför eller varför inte?

2. Varför tror du att det inte finns fler kvinnor inom de högsta chefs-positionerna?

3. Har du någon gång upplevt några hinder för att du är man?

Selektions processen vid anställning av chefer:

- När du skall vara med och utse en ny chef: Hur rekryterar du? Vem/vilka/vad tar du hjälp av när du rekryterar?

- Hur uppfattar du farfars-mormors principen ur ett jämställhets perspektiv? Vad är bra och/eller dåligt med den?

- Varför tror du att ni har farfars-mormors principen?

- Hur blev du chef? *Följdfrågor: Genom att du sökte jobbet eller genom att du blev förfrågad? Hur fick du reda på möjligheten att bli chef? Vart kom den informationen ifrån?*

- Vilken slags person brukar göra karriär som chef tror du? Och alternativt vad för slags person tror du inte skulle lyckas så bra att göra karriär som chef? *Följdfrågor: Typ vilka slags arbete samt vilket slags arbetsstilar är uppskattade respektive vilka arbetsstilar är inte så uppskattade?*

- Vilka egenskaper är viktiga hos en chef?

- Borde verkligen kön (exempel jämnkönsfördelning) spela in i anställnings processen av en ny chef?. Borde inte enbart kompitensen guida?

- I rekryteringsprocessen går ni aktivt ut med att säga att "det är en protering att hitta kvinnliga chefskandidater med kompitens"? Eller tar ni mer rekryteringsprocessen "som den kommer"?

"Projekt mångfald", jämställdhet och mångfald:

Jag har några frågor rörande en artikel jag hittade "Gävle rekryterar inte längre med magkänsla". Artikel handlar om hur mycket fördomar styr över vilka man ansäller. En hel del, visade övningar som chefer i Gävle kommun fick genomföra. Nu har kommunen kvalitetssäkrat sin rekrytering genom både utbildning och ett webbaserat verktyg. *Information: Utbildning i likabehandlings- och diskrimineringsfrågor relaterade till rekryteringsprocessen.*

1.Hur har du använt dig av kunskaperna du fick från "Projekt Mångfald"? *Följdfråga 1: Hur använder du dig av det webbaserade verktyget (som skall vara som stöd för chefer)? Följdfråga 2: Hur har du omsatt kunskaperna du fått från "Projekt Mångfald" i praktiken? Kan du ge några exempel?*

2. Enligt Moa Hjertson, projektledare för "Projekt Mångfald", är den vanligaste fallgropen att man gärna anställer någon som är lik en själv. Hur resonerar du kring rekryteringsprocessen av en ny chef ur ett jämställdhetsperspektiv och mångfaldhetsperspektiv?

3. Många gånger kan mångfald vara en svårighet när man rekryterar nya chefer. Hur gör ni i praktiken vid en rekryterings process för att aktivt öka mångfalden?

51

4. Varför är mångfaldhet viktigt?

5. Varför tror du att socialtjänsten i Gävle har svårt att rekrytera människor med utländsk bakgrund som chefer?

6. Före ni hade "Projekt Mångfald", funderade det dåligt med jämställlhetsarbetet? Var det något som funderade bättre med jämnställdhet innan? *Exempel samspelet mellan män och kvinnor på arbetsplatsen innan ni påbörjade detta projekt?*

7. Kan du ge några praktiska exempel på hur ni omsätter jämställldhetsarbetet i praktiken? *Följdfråga: Är det svårt? Varför eller varför inte?*

8. Kan du gå några praktiska exempel på hur ni omsätter mångfaldsarbetet i praktiken?

9. Har ni något slags uppföljningsarbete för jämställdhets- och mångfaldhetsarbetet?

10. Hur skulle du beskriva mångfalden bland era anställda och era klienter?

Avslut:

1. Kortfattat hur skulle du beskriva din upplevelse på din arbetsplats?

2. Är det något du skulle vilja förändra eller förbättra på din arbetsplats ur ett jämställdhetsperspektiv?

6.2 Appendix 2: Letter of intent

Information jag skall ge innan intervjun börjar:

Jag heter Felicia och går på internationella socialprogrammet på Gävle högskola där jag skriver min c-uppsats. Min metod är intervjua chefer, som dig själv, inom social omsorg. Den övergripande planen är att undersöka organisationskulturen ur ett jämställdhetsperspektiv. Jag har 24 frågor där jag frågar om dina personliga åsikter och erfarenheter, jag har beräknar intervjun att ta 40 minuter. Syftet med intervjun är att få dina personaliga åsikter och uppfattningar rörande ledarskap och jämställdhet. Syftet är inte att få svar som referera tillbaka till var socialtjänsten officiellt står i dessa frågor.

I slutet av intervjun kommer jag även ge dig ett kort frågeformulär, fyra frågor, där jag ber dig uppskatta jämställdheten och hur mycket du upplever du kan påverka ditt arbete. Du kan göra frågeformuläret direkt efter intervjun eller skicka in svaren till mig efter intervjun. Dina svar samt din identitet kommer att **anonymiseras** innan det publiceras. Jag är den enda personen som kommer ha tillgång till ditt namn. Du kommer att refereras i texten som ”Chef X” i mitt arbete. I slutet av intervjun får du gärna skicka in reflektioner efter en vecka eller så. Här nedan är mina kontaktuppgifter. Dina reflektioner kan handla om feedback på metoder, tillägg och frågor. Intervjun kommer att spelas in, du och jag är de enda personerna som har tillgång till denna inspelning. Jag kommer även skicka tillbaka transkripten till dig så att du har möjligheten att läsa igenom samt kommentera om du tycker jag har uppfattar något som felaktigt.